hjbnf
398.21 LOH

W9-BAU-701

DISCARD
PORTER COUNTY
LIBRARY SYSTEM

Loh-Hagan, Virginia, author
Vampires vs. werewolves
33410016548812   03/10/20

DISCARD

PORTER COUNTY
LIBRARY SYSTEM
Hebron Public Library
201 W. Sigler Street
Hebron, IN 46341

VAMPIRES

VS.

WEREWOLVES

Disclaimer:

The creatures in this book are not real. They are from myths. They are fun to imagine. Read the 45th Parallel Press series Magic, Myth, and Mystery to learn more about them.

45TH PARALLEL PRESS

Published in the United States of America by Cherry Lake Publishing
Ann Arbor, Michigan
www.cherrylakepublishing.com

Reading Adviser: Marla Conn, MS, Ed., Literacy specialist, Read-Ability Inc.
Book Designer: Melinda Millward

Photo Credits: © Warpaint/Shutterstock.com, back cover, 15, 16; © Isabell Schatz/Shutterstock.com, cover, 5; © Chorazin3d/Dreamstime.com, cover, 5; © neoblues/istockphoto.com, 6; © Marina Sun/Shutterstock.com, 9; © ArtOfPhotos/Shutterstock.com, 10; © breakermaximus /stock.adobe.com, 12; © losw/Shutterstock.com, 19; © GraphicsRF/Shutterstock.com, 19, 20; © vectortatu/Shutterstock.com, 20; © Unholy Vault Designs/Shutterstock.com, 21; © rudall30/Shutterstock.com, 23, 24; © Marina Keremkhanova/Shutterstock.com, 25; © THEPALMER/istockphoto.com, 25; © Ricardo Reitmeyer/Shutterstock.com, 27; © serpeblu/Shutterstock.com, 29

Graphic Element Credits: © studiostoks/Shutterstock.com, back cover, multiple interior pages; © infostocker/ Shutterstock.com, back cover, multiple interior pages; © mxbfilms/Shutterstock.com, front cover; © MF production/Shutterstock.com, front cover, multiple interior pages; © AldanNi/Shutterstock.com, front cover, multiple interior pages; © Andrii Symonenko/Shutterstock.com, front cover, multiple interior pages; © acidmit/ Shutterstock.com, front cover, multiple interior pages; © manop/Shutterstock.com, multiple interior pages; © Lina Kalina/Shutterstock.com, multiple interior pages; © mejorana/Shutterstock.com, multiple interior pages; © NoraVector/Shutterstock.com, multiple interior pages; © Smirnov Viacheslav/Shutterstock.com, multiple interior pages; © Piotr Urakau/Shutterstock.com, multiple interior pages; © IMOGI graphics/Shutterstock.com, multiple interior pages; © jirawat phueksriphan/Shutterstock.com, multiple interior pages

Copyright © 2020 by Cherry Lake Publishing

All rights reserved. No part of this book may be reproduced or utilized
in any form or by any means without written permission from the publisher.

45th Parallel Press is an imprint of Cherry Lake Publishing.

Library of Congress Cataloging-in-Publication Data

Names: Loh-Hagan, Virginia, author.
Title: Vampires vs. werewolves / by Virginia Loh-Hagan.
Other titles: Vampires versus werewolves
Description: Ann Arbor, Michigan : Cherry Lake Publishing, 2020. |
    Series: Battle royale : lethal warriors | Includes index.
Identifiers: LCCN 2019032870 | ISBN 9781534159310 (hardcover) | ISBN 9781534161610 (paperback) |
    ISBN 9781534160460 (pdf) | ISBN 9781534162761 (ebook)
Subjects: LCSH: Vampires–Juvenile literature. | Werewolves–Juvenile literature.
Classification: LCC GR830.V3 L643 2020 | DDC 398.21–dc23
LC record available at https://lccn.loc.gov/2019032870

Printed in the United States of America
Corporate Graphics

About the Author

Dr. Virginia Loh-Hagan is an author, university professor, and former classroom teacher. She lives like a vampire because she works at night and sleeps during the day. She's also constantly battling her own bloodthirsty beasts (known as Woody and Dotty). She lives in San Diego with her very tall husband and very naughty dogs. To learn more about her, visit www.virginialoh.com.

Table of Contents

Introduction...4

Vampires.. 6

Werewolves... 12

Choose Your Battleground.................... 18

Fight On!..22

And the Victor Is. 28

Consider This!..32
Learn More!..32
Glossary 32
Index 32

Introduction

Imagine a battle between vampires and werewolves. Who would win? Who would lose?

Enter the world of *Battle Royale: Lethal* **Warriors**! Warriors are fighters. This is a fight to the death! The last team standing is the **victor**! Victors are winners. They get to live.

Opponents are fighters who compete against each other. They challenge each other. They fight with everything they've got. They use weapons. They use their special skills. They use their powers.

They're not fighting for prizes. They're not fighting for honor. They're fighting for their lives. Victory is their only option.

Let the games begin!

VS.

VAMPIRES

Vampires sleep in dark places.
Some sleep in coffins.

Vampires are bloodthirsty **undead** creatures. The undead are dead. But they act alive. Vampires were once human. Then, they became **demons**. Demons are monsters. They sleep during the day. They hunt at night. They have "the hunger." They crave blood.

There are different types of vampires. Strigoi are the most common. They're also the most dangerous. They're **immortal**. This means they live forever. They're evil. They're strong hunters and killers.

Vampires live in **covens**. Covens are vampire groups. There are usually 3 to 4 vampires in a coven. They hunt together. They feed together. They're led by a vampire prince.

Vampires kill to eat. They have powerful **fangs**. Fangs are sharp teeth. Vampires have superpowers. They're stronger than 10 men. They're good fighters. They climb walls. They run fast. They jump high. They fly. They hear well. They smell well. They see well. They have **night vision**. They see in total darkness. They see heat. They track prey. They have long, thick nails. They grab and slash. They talk through **telepathy**. They read minds. They talk without saying words out loud.

They have super healing powers. They regrow their fangs. They regrow body parts. They don't get hurt easily. They don't get human sicknesses. They never get tired. They're also smart. They can control minds.

Some vampires live in castles.

Vampires are hard to kill. But they can be killed. Staking kills them. Wooden **stakes** are pointy sticks. They cut through vampires' hearts.

Vampires hate all pure things. They hate churches. They hate crosses. They hate water. They hate silver. All these things burn their skin. Sunlight also burns their skin. It can cause vampires to burst into flames. Vampires will turn to ashes. That's why they sleep during the day.

Vampires can't have babies. To build armies, vampires must turn people into vampires. They let humans drink their blood. The turning process is painful. It lasts 3 days. Humans get sick. They slip into a deep sleep. Some die. Others wake up as vampires.

FUN FACTS ABOUT VAMPIRES

- The Black Death happened around the 1350s. It killed millions of people in Europe. Victims had blood coming out of their mouths. People thought they were vampires. When they died, people put rocks or bricks in their mouths. This was meant to stop them from coming back to life.

- Sekhmet was an Egyptian goddess. She may have been a vampire. She was called Lady of the Bloodbath. Ra was the sun god. He sent for Sekhmet to punish humans. Sekhmet killed a lot of people. She drank their blood. Ra changed his mind. He wanted to save some humans. He tricked Sekhmet. He gave her a red drink. Sekhmet thought it was blood. The drink made her sleepy. Sekhmet stopped killing.

- Penanggalan are vampires from Southeast Asian stories. They are flying female heads. Their guts dangle below their heads. They use their long tongues to lap up blood. Their main victims are pregnant women and young children.

WEREWOLVES

Full moons have a lot of power.
Werewolves are drawn to them.

Werewolves are humans. They're **shapeshifters**. This means they change shapes. They change from humans to werewolves. Werewolves are super strong and powerful wolves.

They shift during full moons. But the top dogs can shift whenever they want. Newer werewolves need to learn to do this. They can only shift during full moons. The shifting process is quick. But it's hard and painful. Bones break. They grow longer. They change shape. They move. They burst through skin. Skin changes. Organs move around. Muscles move around. Fur sprouts out. Skulls change shape. Werewolves are the weakest when shifting. They're tired. They're confused.

Werewolves are strong hunters. They're built to kill. They have sharp claws. They have sharp teeth. They tear limbs. They rip flesh. They crack bones. They rip doors. They have thick bodies. They ram. They dent steel.

They have super strength. They run far. They run fast. They move gracefully. They climb. They jump. They have **stamina**. This means they don't get tired.

Werewolves have super senses. They see well. They have night vision. They hear well. They smell well. They smell 100 times better than vampires.

They also have super healing powers. They heal fast. They're **immune** to sicknesses. Immune means they're not affected.

Werewolves are territorial. This means they protect their space.

Werewolves hunt and fight as a **pack**. A pack is a wolf family. They talk. They howl. They listen for echoes. This makes them better hunters. They trap prey. They circle prey. They attack as a pack.

A werewolf bite is dangerous. It can kill vampires. It can turn humans into werewolves. Unlike vampires, werewolves can have babies. They can add to their packs.

Werewolves have weaknesses. They don't live forever. But they age slowly. They hate silver. Silver will weaken them by burning their insides. **Quicksilver** will kill them. It's liquid mercury. It's poisonous.

FUN FACTS ABOUT WEREWOLVES

- A werewoman is a female shapeshifter. She doesn't have to be a wolf. She can be any animal. She uses the same changing process as a werewolf. In African stories, it's common for werewomen to become hyenas or leopards.

- Some Eastern European legends feature dead werewolves becoming vampires. The Slavic word for werewolf is *volkodlak*. It means "vampire" in the Serbian language.

- Scandinavian Vikings told werewolf stories. Vikings are Norse warriors. Ulfhednars were warriors. They dressed up in wolf skins. They painted their skins black. They took on the spirit of the wolf. They fought like wolves in battle. They howled. They went crazy. They acted wild.

- In Armenian stories, women who commit sins have to spend 7 years as wolves. They turn into wolves at night. They crave human meat. They eat their own children. Then, they eat other people's children. In the day, they become humans again. They're upset by what they did.

CHOOSE YOUR BATTLEGROUND

Vampires and werewolves are fierce fighters. They're well-matched. They both have similar powers. But they have different ways of fighting. They also have different weaknesses. They're natural enemies. They hate each other. So, choose your battleground carefully!

Battleground #1: Sea

• In general, vampires don't like water. They can't cross running water. Water also acts like a mirror. Vampires don't like mirrors. They have no soul. So, they can't see their reflections.

• Werewolves would be comfortable in a sea battle. They're excellent swimmers. But they don't like salt. The sea is made of saltwater. The salt burns their eyes and noses.

In some stories, werewolves protect humans from vampires.

Battleground #2: Land

• Vampires are used to fighting on land. However, they would need to keep away from garlic crops. Vampires hate garlic. Garlic has a strong smell. It makes vampires sick. Open land is okay for vampires. But buildings are tricky. Vampires have to be invited into buildings.

• Werewolves have no problem fighting on land. This gives them more room to run.

Battleground #3: Mountains

• Vampires can fly. They would be able to reach mountain heights easily. They also aren't affected by cold weather.

• Werewolves prefer mountains, woods, and forests. They sleep in caves. They can run and climb over rocks. They know how to cover their tracks. They just need to stay away from wolfsbane. Wolfsbane is a plant. It has deadly poison. It grows on mountains.

Vampires: Vampires' best weapon is their fangs. They use fangs to bite into victims. The sharp teeth quickly cut through skin. Vampires hold victims in their mouths. They suck out their blood. Vampire fangs act like needles. They have a small hole at the tip. They have a long tube inside. They draw out blood from the victim. Fangs are popular symbols for killers and hunters.

Werewolves: Werewolves also have strong teeth. But their best weapon is their jaws. Their jaws are super powerful. They can rip flesh. They can crush bones. They have strong grips. They can apply a lot of crushing pressure. This means they can chomp through anything in a couple of bites. Werewolves don't chew their food. They saw meat off with their teeth. They swallow big chunks of meat. They leave little waste. They eat every part of their prey.

FIGHT ON!

The battle begins! The sun has gone down. It's nighttime. Vampires and werewolves circle each other. As hunters, they're watching their prey. It's pretty quiet, for now.

Move 1:

Werewolves herd vampires into the center. Vampires stand with their backs to each other. They make sure to keep their eyes on the werewolves. The werewolves surround the vampires. They form 2 circles around them. There's an inner circle. There's an outer circle. There are more werewolves than vampires. Packs are larger than covens.

Both vampires and werewolves try to stay hidden from humans.

Move 2:

Vampires need to get out of this trap. Werewolves are slowly closing in on them. They're taking their time. They know they can do this all night. They can do this until the sun comes up. The vampires talk to each other with telepathy. They agree to fly away at the same time. They leap up into the air. This movement starts the frenzy.

Move 3:

Werewolves jump. They claw at the vampires. Some vampires get away. Some get dragged down. The ones that get dragged down are on the ground. Pack members pounce. They hold the vampires down. They tear. They open their mouths to bite down.

Dying werewolves shift back to human form. They die as humans.

Vampires: Vampires need blood to survive. They'll die without blood. They prefer fresh blood. They prefer human blood. But they'll drink animal blood if they have to. Blood represents the source of life. It gives vampires power. It restores their bodies. It heals their wounds. It keeps their bodies from rotting. Remember, vampires are dead. Fresh blood moves through their bodies. This keeps their flesh alive. Vampires need to drink a couple of times a week. Wounded vampires need to drink more.

Werewolves: Werewolves eat everything. They're not picky eaters. They need to eat all the time. They spend most of their time hunting. Their favorite food is fresh raw meat. They usually eat the meat of big animals. They don't really like to eat humans. But they will if needed. They eat twice as much as their body weight.

Move 4:

The vampires that flew away come to help. They pick up the werewolves. They throw them off their vampire friends. They throw them hard. They break bones. But there are a lot of werewolves. Vampires use telepathy to tell other covens to come help.

Move 5:

Werewolves continue to circle around again. They howl for more packs to come. Vampires need to act quickly. They need to separate the pack. They fly away in different directions. They are fast enough to get a head start. But the werewolves are quick to catch up.

Some vampires can turn into bats.

27

AND THE VICTOR IS . . .

What are their next moves?

Who do you think would win?

Vampires could win if:

- They cover up their smell. They should be aware of the wind. Winds carry scents. Werewolves can smell them from miles away.
- They avoid the full moon. This is when werewolves are at their strongest. Plus, there will be more werewolves during full moons. Vampires should avoid fighting packs.

Werewolves could win if:

- They fight as a pack. They gang up on prey that is alone.
- They can trap vampires at a crossroads or at a holy place. Vampires are weak around crosses.
- They keep vampires busy until the sun comes up. They'll turn back into humans. But vampires will die.

Vampires and werewolves live cursed lives.

Vampires: Top Champion

Lilith was from Jewish stories. She was thought to be the mother of vampires. Her name meant "night monster." Lilith was the first woman. God made Adam and Lilith from the same soil. Lilith was Adam's first wife. She thought she was Adam's equal. She refused to obey him. So, Adam left her. God made Eve from Adam's rib. Lilith was not happy about this. She became a demon. She had monsters for children. God sent angels to bring her back. She didn't want to go. She was punished. Her children were killed. She vowed to kill humans. She hunted humans. She did this at night. She stole babies. She stole children. She drank their blood. She ate them.

Werewolves: Top Champion

Werewolves appeared in Greek myths. Lycaon was the son of Pelasgus. Some people think Pelasgus was the first man. Lycaon was the king of Arcadia. He was mean and cruel. Zeus was the king of the Greek gods. He went to Lycaon's house for dinner. Lycaon wanted to trick Zeus. He wanted to test him. He wanted to see if he was really all-knowing. So, Lycaon killed his son, Nyctimus. He wanted to see if Zeus would find out. This made Zeus mad. Zeus brought Nyctimus back to life. He punished Lycaon. He flooded Lycaon's lands. He turned Lycaon into a wolf. Lycaon had about 50 sons. Zeus turned all his sons into wolves as well. This started the curse of the werewolves.

Consider This!

THINK ABOUT IT!

- How are vampires and werewolves alike? How are they different? Are they more alike or different? Why do you think so?
- Read the 45th Parallel Press books about vampires and werewolves. What more did you learn about these monsters?
- Would you rather be a vampire or werewolf? Explain your answer.
- What skills do you have to fight a vampire? What skills do you have to fight a werewolf?
- There are many movies and books about vampires and werewolves. Make a list of the ones you have read or seen. Which one is your favorite? Why? How did the story change the myths about vampires and werewolves?

LEARN MORE!

- Bingham, Jane. *Vampires and Werewolves*. Chicago, IL: Raintree, 2014.
- Klepeis, Alicia Z. *Vampires: The Truth Behind History's Creepiest Bloodsuckers*. Mankato, MN: Capstone Press, 2015.
- McCollum, Sean. *Werewolves: The Truth Behind History's Scariest Shape-Shifters*. Mankato, MN: Capstone Press, 2015.
- O'Hearn, Michael. *Vampires vs Werewolves*. Mankato, MN: Capstone Press, 2012.

GLOSSARY

covens (KUH-venz) groups of vampires or witches
demons (DEE-muhnz) monsters
fangs (FANGZ) sharp, pointy teeth
immortal (ih-MOR-tuhl) being able to live forever
immune (ih-MYOON) being resistant or not being affected
night vision (NITE VIZH-uhn) having the ability to see in the dark
opponents (uh-POH-nuhnts) fighters who compete against each other
pack (PAK) a small group
quicksilver (KWIK-sil-vur) liquid mercury
shapeshifters (SHAYP-shift-urz) beings that have the ability to change shapes or forms

stakes (STAYKS) wooden posts with pointy tips
stamina (STAM-uh-nuh) the ability to keep going and not get tired
telepathy (tuh-LEP-uh-thee) ability to talk to others without speaking
undead (uhn-DED) creatures who are dead but animated like vampires, zombies, and mummies
victor (VIK-tur) the winner
Vikings (VYE-kingz) Norse warriors
warriors (WOR-ee-urz) fighters

INDEX

battlegrounds, 18–20
battles, 22–27

fangs, 8, 21
food, 25

jaws, 21

Lilith, 30
Lycaon, 31

shapeshifters, 13, 17

vampires, 6–11, 30
  battlegrounds, 18–20
  battles, 22–27
  food, 25
  fun facts, 11
  how they win, 28
  powers, 8, 13, 14
  and sleep, 6, 7
  types of, 7
  weapons, 21
  what they hate, 10

victors, 4, 28–29

weapons, 21
werewolves, 12–17, 31
  battlegrounds, 18–20
  battles, 22–27
  food, 25
  fun facts, 17
  how they win, 29
  powers, 16
  weaknesses, 16
  weapons, 21